MILAN SHOPPING GUIDE 2022
Best Rated Stores in Milan, Italy

© Andrea Y. Weidman
© E.G.P. Editorial

ISBN-13: 9798504951478

Copyright ©
All rights reserved.

MILAN SHOPPING GUIDE
Most Recommended Stores in the City

*This directory is dedicated to the Business Owners and Managers
who provide the experience that the locals and tourists enjoy.
Thanks you very much for all that you do and thank for being the "People Choice".*

*Thanks to everyone that posts their reviews online and
the amazing reviews sites that make our life easier.*

*The places listed in this book are the most positively reviewed
and recommended by locals and travelers from around the world.*

*Thank you for your time and enjoy the directory that is
designed with locals and tourist in mind!*

TOP 500 SHOPPING SPOTS

The Most Recommended
(from #1 to #500)

Milan Shopping Guide / The Most Recommended Stores in the City

---

#1
Matia's Fashion Outlet
Category: Outlet Stores, Fashion
Average Price: Modest
Area: Palestro
Address: Corso Venezia 37
20121 Milan Italy
Phone: 02 76281300

#2
Esselunga
Category: Shopping Centers, Grocery
Average Price: Modest
Area: Porta Romana
Address: Via Carlo De Angeli 1
20141 Milan Italy
Phone: 02 56816062

#3
Zap Milano
Category: Outlet Stores, Accessories, Women's Clothing
Average Price: Expensive
Area: Ortomercato
Address: Via Quintiliano 33
20138 Milan Italy
Phone: 02 58016368

#4
Centro Piazza Lodi
Category: Shopping Centers
Average Price: Modest
Area: Porta Vittoria
Address: Viale Umbria 4
20135 Milan Italy
Phone: 02 540451

#5
Outlet Bassetti
Category: Outlet Stores
Average Price: Inexpensive
Area: Monumentale
Address: Via Procaccini 32
20154 Milan Italy
Phone: 02 3450125

#6
Carrefour Market
Category: Shopping Centers
Average Price: Modest
Area: Parco Sempione
Address: Via Vincenzo Monti 55
20123 Milan Italy
Phone: 02 4694107

#7
Centro Commerciale Vulcano
Category: Shopping Centers
Average Price: Modest
Area: Sesto San Giovanni
Address: Viale Italia 555
20099 Sesto San Giovanni Italy
Phone: 02 22476426

#8
La Rinascente
Category: Department Stores
Average Price: Expensive
Area: Centro Storico
Address: Piazza Del Duomo
20121 Milan Italy
Phone: 02 88521

#9
Aumai
Category: Discount Store, Shopping Centers
Average Price: Inexpensive
Area: Turro Gorla Greco
Address: Via Emilio De Marchi 10
20125 Milan Italy
Phone: 039 6185326

#10
Mercato Comunale Wagner
Category: Shopping Centers
Average Price: Modest
Area: Fiera
Address: Piazza Wagner 4
20145 Milan Italy
Phone: 02 0200

#11
Salvagente
Category: Outlet Stores, Men's Clothing, Women's Clothing
Average Price: Modest
Area: Porta Vittoria
Address: Via Fratelli Bronzetti 16
20129 Milan Italy
Phone: 02 76110328

#12
Di Mano In Mano
Category: Vintage & Consignment
Average Price: Modest
Area: Certosa
Address: Viale Carlo Espinasse
9720156 Milan Italy
Phone: 02 33400800

Milan Shopping Guide / The Most Recommended Stores in the City

---

#13
Piazza Portello
Category: Shopping Centers
Average Price: Modest
Area: Certosa
Address: Via Grosotto 7
20149 Milan Italy
Phone: 02 33005170

#14
Bicocca Village
Category: Shopping Centers
Average Price: Modest
Area: Bicocca
Address: Viale Sarca
20126 Milan Italy
Phone: 02 66101276

#15
Vintage Shop
Category: Antiques, Used,
Vintage & Consignment
Average Price: Modest
Area: Porta Genova
Address: Alzaia Naviglio Pavese 52
20143 Milan Italy
Phone: 02 89415559

#16
Centro Sarca
Category: Shopping Centers
Average Price: Modest
Area: Bicocca
Address: Via Milanese 10
20099 Sesto San Giovanni Italy
Phone: 02 2412431

#17
Maglieria Tina
Category: Men's Clothing,
Women's Clothing, Lingerie
Average Price: Modest
Area: Porta Vittoria
Address: Via Tito Livio 24
20137 Milan Italy
Phone: 02 55188156

#18
Esselunga
Category: Shopping Centers, Grocery
Average Price: Modest
Area: Washington
Address: Via Giorgio Washington 53
20146 Milan Italy
Phone: 02 48102631

#19
City Outlet
Category: Shoe Stores
Average Price: Modest
Area: Palestro
Address: Via Vittorio Veneto,
2020124 Milan Italy
Phone: 02 36598429

#20
10 Corso Como
Category: Fashion, Outlet Stores
Average Price: Exclusive
Area: Moscova
Address: Via Tazzoli 3
20154 Milan Italy
Phone: 02 29015130

#21
W Milano
Category: Home Decor, Used,
Vintage & Consignment
Average Price: Modest
Area: Washington
Address: Via Giorgio Washington 51
20146 Milan Italy
Phone: 02 87386401

#22
Oviesse
Category: Shopping Centers
Average Price: Modest
Area: Porta Vittoria
Address: Viale Umbria 4
20135 Milan Italy
Phone: 02 54116672

#23
Surplus Corso Garibaldi
Category: Women's Clothing, Men's Clothing
Average Price: Modest
Area: Moscova
Address: Corso Garibaldi 7
20121 Milan Italy
Phone: 02 72023422

#24
Emporio Isola
Category: Shoe Stores, Men's Clothing,
Women's Clothing
Average Price: Modest
Area: Parco Sempione
Address: Via Prina 11
20154 Milan Italy
Phone: 02 3491040

Milan Shopping Guide / The Most Recommended Stores in the City

#25
Made In The Shade
Category: Fashion
Average Price: Exclusive
Area: Porta Genova
Address: Ripa Di Porta Ticinese, 53
20143 Milan Italy
Phone: 02 58118785

#26
Meet2biz
Category: Women's Clothing, Men's Clothing
Average Price: Modest
Area: Porta Genova
Address: Alzaia Naviglio Grande 14
20144 Milan Italy
Phone: 02 36592334

#27
Liu Jo
Category: Women's Clothing
Average Price: Modest
Area: Buenos Aires
Address: Corso Buenos Aires, 40
20124 Milan Italy
Phone: 02 29537080

#28
COIN
Category: Men's Clothing, Women's Clothing, Lingerie
Average Price: Modest
Area: Centro Storico
Address: Piazza Cantore 12
20123 Milan Italy
Phone: 02 58104385

#29
Lila
Category: Women's Clothing, Jewelry
Average Price: Modest
Area: Porta Genova
Address: Via Vigevano 11
20144 Milan Italy
Phone: 02 8323073

#30
Coin
Category: Shopping Centers, Grocery
Average Price: Expensive
Area: Centro Storico
Address: Piazza Cinque Giornate 1A
20129 Milan Italy
Phone: 02 55192083

#31
Double B - Brian & Barry Outlet
Category: Fashion, Outlet Stores
Average Price: Modest
Area: Monumentale
Address: Viale Lancetti, 28
20158 Milan Italy
Phone: 02 69901193

#33
Trend
Category: Men's Clothing, Women's Clothing, Children's Clothing
Average Price: Modest
Area: Centro Storico
Address: Via Torino 46
20123 Milan Italy
Phone: 02 8052813

#32
OVS
Category: Department Stores
Average Price: Modest
Area: Fiera
Address: Via Arona 15
20149 Milan Italy
Phone: 02 314543

#34
Mauro Leone
Category: Shoe Stores
Average Price: Modest
Area: Centro Storico
Address: Corso Di Porta Ticinese 103
20123 Milan Italy
Phone: 02 58105041

#35
Belfiore
Category: Shoe Stores
Average Price: Expensive
Area: Fiera
Address: Via Belfiore 9
20145 Milan Italy
Phone: 02 468042

#36
Temporary Store
Category: Home Services, Accessories, Women's Clothing
Average Price: Modest
Area: Porta Genova, Centro Storico
Address: Via Vigevano 120144 Milan Italy
Phone: 02 39529202

Milan Shopping Guide / The Most Recommended Stores in the City

---

#37
Target
Category: Home Decor, Gift Shops
Average Price: Modest
Area: Centro Storico
Address: Corso Di Porta Ticinese 1
20123 Milan Italy
Phone: 02 876692

#38
Boggi Factory Store
Category: Men's Clothing, Outlet Stores
Average Price: Modest
Area: Monumentale
Address: Viale Lancetti 28
20158 Milan Italy
Phone: 02 69901207

#39
Esselunga
Category: Shopping Centers, Grocery
Average Price: Modest
Area: Palestro
Address: Viale Piave 38
20129 Milan Italy
Phone: 02 2047871

#40
Wok
Category: Women's Clothing
Average Price: Modest
Area: Porta Romana
Address: Viale Col
20136 Milan Italy
Phone: 02 89829700

#41
High Tech
Category: Home Decor, Gift Shops
Average Price: Expensive
Area: Moscova
Address: Piazza XXV Aprile 1220128
Milan Italy
Phone: 02 62411058

#42
Colazione Da Miny
Category: Accessories, Leather Goods
Average Price: Inexpensive
Area: Porta Genova
Address: Viale Coni Zugna 55
20123 Milan Italy
Phone: 333 2108883

#43
Lidl
Category: Discount Store
Average Price: Modest
Area: Certosa
Address: Via Giovanni Da Udine
2820156 Milan Italy
Phone: 8004 80048

#44
Matia's Fashion Outlet
Category: Fashion, Outlet Stores
Average Price: Modest
Area: Moscova
Address: Piazza Carlo Mirabello 4
20121 Milan Italy
Phone: 02 62694535

#45
Iper La Grande I
Category: Shopping Centers
Average Price: Modest
Area: Certosa
Address: Piazza Portello
20149 Milan Italy
Phone: 02 392591

#46
L'outlet Del Kasalingo
Category: Outlet Stores
Average Price: Modest
Area: Bovisa
Address: Piazza Bausan
20158 Milan Italy
Phone: 02 39314108

#47
Fashion Discount
Category: Women's Clothing
Average Price: Modest
Area: Washington
Address: Corso Magenta, 56
20123 Milan Italy
Phone: 334 8953103

#48
Stradivarius
Category: Women's Clothing, Accessories
Average Price: Modest
Area: Palestro
Address: Via Lazzaro Palazzi 2
20124 Milan Italy
Phone: 02 29514796

Milan Shopping Guide / The Most Recommended Stores in the City

---

#49
Chanel
Category: Accessories, Women's Clothing
Average Price: Exclusive
Area: Centro Storico
Address: Via Sant'andrea 10A
20121 Milan Italy
Phone: 02 76016545

#50
Sakurasan
Category: Accessories, Women's Clothing
Average Price: Modest
Area: Porta Vittoria
Address: Viale Lazio, 6
20135 Milan Italy
Phone: 02 5516745

#51
Coop
Category: Shopping Centers, Grocery
Average Price: Modest
Area: Fiera
Address: Via Arona 15
20149 Milan Italy
Phone: 02 3182821

#52
Zara Italia
Category: Men's Clothing
Average Price: Expensive
Area: Porta Genova
Address: Via Morimondo 26
20143 Milan Italy
Phone: 02 8180081

#53
Bastard Store
Category: Sports Wear, Shoe Stores
Average Price: Expensive
Area: Ospedale Maggiore
Address: Via Scipio Slataper 19
20125 Milan Italy
Phone: 02 40708233

#54
Guendalina
Category: Women's Clothing
Average Price: Modest
Area: Centro Storico
Address: Corso Di Porta Ticinese
6520123 Milan Italy
Phone: 02 58113545

#55
Upim
Category: Shopping Centers
Average Price: Expensive
Area: Stazione Centrale
Address: Corso Buenos Aires 21
20124 Milan Italy
Phone: 02 9521352

#56
Manganini
Category: Fashion
Average Price: Modest
Area: Affori
Address: Via Astesani
Alessandro, 820161 Milan Italy
Phone: 02 6457300

#57
Scout
Category: Men's Clothing, Women's Clothing
Average Price: Modest
Area: Centro Storico
Address: Corso Di Porta Ticinese 12
20123 Milan Italy
Phone: 02 87088048

#58
Chicchi Ginepri
Category: Men's Clothing, Women's Clothing
Average Price: Modest
Area: Fiera
Address: Viale Murillo 23
20149 Milan Italy
Phone: 02 4035598

#59
Lidl
Category: Grocery, Discount Store
Average Price: Inexpensive
Area: Ospedale Maggiore
Address: Via Valassina 12
20159 Milan Italy
Phone: 02 66823263

#60
Blume Atelier
Category: Women's Clothing
Average Price: Modest
Area: Porta Genova
Address: Via Delle Foppette 2
20144 Milan Italy
Phone: 02 39566153

Milan Shopping Guide / The Most Recommended Stores in the City

#61
Arredamenti Piemonti
Category: Outlet Stores
Average Price: Expensive
Area: Bovisa
Address: Via Bovisasca
20158 Milan Italy
Phone: 02 39324249

#62
OVS
Category: Department Stores
Average Price: Expensive
Area: Stazione Centrale
Address: Corso Buenos Aires 35
20124 Milan Italy
Phone: 02 20404801

#63
Allegra Unione
Category: Women's Clothing
Average Price: Modest
Area: Washington
Address: MM Cadorna
20123 Milan Italy
Phone: 02 86460302

#64
Figus Designer
Category: Jewelry, Leather Goods, Accessories
Average Price: Modest
Area: Centro Storico
Address: Corso Magenta 31
20123 Milan Italy
Phone: 02 86450155

#65
Fashion Park
Category: Personal Shopping
Average Price: Modest
Area: Parco Sempione
Address: Via Bertani 16
20154 Milan Italy
Phone: 02 89052569

#66
Carpe Diem
Category: Accessories, Home Decor
Average Price: Expensive
Area: Palestro
Address: Viale Tunisia 1
20124 Milan Italy
Phone: 02 29517833

#67
OVS
Category: Children's Clothing, Men's Clothing, Women's Clothing
Average Price: Modest
Area: Ospedale Maggiore
Address: Via Moncalieri 15
20162 Milan Italy
Phone: 02 6438297

#68
Dressai
Category: Women's Clothing, Luggage
Average Price: Modest
Area: Washington
Address: Piazza Giovanni Antonio Bazzi 220144 Milan Italy
Phone: 348 4818322

#69
Humana Vintage
Category: Used, Vintage & Consignment
Average Price: Modest
Area: Centro Storico
Address: Via Cappellari 3
20123 Milan Italy
Phone: 02 72080606

#70
Now
Category: Gift Shops
Average Price: Modest
Area: Porta Romana
Address: Viale Sabotino
2020135 Milan Italy
Phone: 02 58309976

#71
Dufry - Free Shop
Category: Shopping Centers, Grocery
Average Price: Modest
Area: Turro Gorla Greco
Address: Via Giovanni Battista Sammartini, 420125 Milan Italy
Phone: 02 6697322

#72
Tiger
Category: Home Decor, Party Supplies
Average Price: Inexpensive
Area: Centro Storico
Address: Via Meravigli 1
20123 Milan Italy
Phone: 02 89096708

Milan Shopping Guide / The Most Recommended Stores in the City

#73
Giorgio Armani
Category: Women's Clothing, Men's Clothing
Average Price: Exclusive
Area: Centro Storico
Address: Via Alessandro Manzoni 31
20121 Milan Italy
Phone: 02 6572401

#74
Coin
Category: Shopping Centers
Average Price: Expensive
Area: Washington
Address: Corso Vercelli 30-32
20145 Milan Italy
Phone: 02 43990001

#75
Iuter
Category: Women's Clothing, Men's Clothing, Accessories
Average Price: Modest
Area: Centro Storico
Address: Corso Di Porta Ticinese 48
20123 Milan Italy
Phone: 02 84253390

#76
Skylab Outlet
Category: Outlet Stores, Accessories, Women's Clothing
Average Price: Modest
Area: Centro Storico
Address: Corso Di Porta Romana 50
20122 Milan Italy
Phone: 02 58324691

#77
Biffi Boutique
Category: Men's Clothing, Women's Clothing
Average Price: Expensive
Area: Centro Storico
Address: Corso Genova 5
20123 Milan Italy
Phone: 02 83116052

#78
Shabby Chic
Category: Used, Vintage & Consignment
Average Price: Modest
Area: Porta Vittoria
Address: Via Benvenuto Cellini
2120129 Milan Italy
Phone: 02 76018149

#79
Paolo Tonali
Category: Women's Clothing
Average Price: Modest
Area: Washington
Address: Via Giosuè Carducci 12
20123 Milan Italy
Phone: 02 36566920

#80
Alviero Martini Factory Outlet
Category: Fashion, Outlet Stores
Average Price: Modest
Area: Porta Vittoria
Address: Via Muratori 13
20135 Milan Italy
Phone: 02 599901

#81
Highline
Category: Outlet Stores
Average Price: Inexpensive
Area: Centro Storico
Address: Corso Vittorio Emanuele II 28
20122 Milan Italy
Phone: 02 76014870

#82
The Highline Outlet
Category: Accessories, Men's Clothing, Women's Clothing
Average Price: Modest
Area: Centro Storico
Address: Corso Vittorio Emanuele II 30
20122 Milan Italy
Phone: 02 76014870

#83
Bottega Velasca
Category: Shoe Stores
Average Price: Modest
Area: Parco Sempione
Address: Piazza Sempione 2
20154 Milan Italy
Phone: 02 92861813

#84
Zara
Category: Men's Clothing, Women's Clothing
Average Price: Modest
Area: Centro Storico
Address: Via Torino 2
20123 Milan Italy
Phone: 02 89095047

Milan Shopping Guide / The Most Recommended Stores in the City

---

#85
Tutto A Mezz'Euro E Più
Category: Home Decor, Accessories
Average Price: Modest
Area: Porta Romana
Address: Corso San Gottardo 18
20136 Milan Italy
Phone: 02 83390223

#86
Dictionary
Category: Women's Clothing, Men's Clothing
Average Price: Expensive
Area: Centro Storico
Address: Corso Di Porta Ticinese 46
20123 Milan Italy
Phone: 02 8358212

#87
Bazaar Della Lana
Category: Women's Clothing
Average Price: Modest
Area: Porta Romana
Address: Corso Lodi 24
20135 Milan Italy
Phone: 02 54107528

#88
Lidl
Category: Department Stores
Average Price: Modest
Area: Washington
Address: Viale Ergisto Bezzi 69
20146 Milan Italy
Phone: 8004 80048

#89
Luisa Spagnoli
Category: Women's Clothing
Average Price: Modest
Area: Stazione Centrale
Address: Corso Buenos Aires, 39
20124 Milan Italy
Phone: 02 29537033

#90
Docksmart
Category: Outlet Stores
Average Price: Modest
Area: Ortomercato
Address: Via Toffetti,
920139 Milan Italy
Phone: 02 55213641

#91
Pracchi Discount
Category: Shopping Centers, Grocery
Average Price: Modest
Area: Porta Vittoria
Address: Viale Umbria 66
20135 Milan Italy
Phone: 02 55195980

#92
Mas Que Nada
Category: Women's Clothing
Average Price: Expensive
Area: Porta Romana
Address: Corso Lodi, 12
20135 Milan Italy
Phone: 02 58312596

#93
Campania30
Category: Antiques, Jewelry
Average Price: Modest
Area: Porta Vittoria
Address: Viale Campania 30
20133 Milan Italy
Phone: 02 70011999

#94
Terranova
Category: Men's Clothing, Women's Clothing
Average Price: Modest
Area: Centro Storico
Address: Via Torino 61
20123 Milan Italy
Phone: 02 89011736

#95
Original Marines
Category: Children's Clothing
Average Price: Modest
Area: Washington
Address: Vie Lorenteggio 25
20146 Milan Italy
Phone: 02 427292

#96
Caramelle
Category: Shoe Stores
Average Price: Modest
Area: Città Studi
Address: Piazza Gobetti,
1420131 Milan Italy
Phone: 02 26681951

Milan Shopping Guide / The Most Recommended Stores in the City

#97
Anna Fabiano
Category: Fashion, Personal Shopping
Average Price: Exclusive
Area: Centro Storico
Address: C. Di Porta Ticinese,
4020123 Milan Italy
Phone: 02 58112348

#98
Salvatore + Marie
Category: Accessories, Home Decor
Average Price: Expensive
Area: Porta Genova
Address: Via Vigevano 33
20144 Milan Italy
Phone: 02 89422152

#99
Tanagra
Category: Shoe Stores
Average Price: Modest
Area: Centro Storico
Address: Via Torino 48
20123 Milan Italy
Phone: 02 8057052

#100
Figus Designer
Category: Jewelry, Leather Goods
Average Price: Modest
Area: Moscova
Address: Corso Garibaldi 46
20121 Milan Italy
Phone: 02 86450155

#101
L'Outlet Dell'occhiale
Category: Outlet Stores, Eyewear & Opticians
Average Price: Inexpensive
Area: Washington
Address: Via Tagiura 16
20146 Milan Italy
Phone: 02 43126471

#102
Oviesse Outlet
Category: Outlet Stores
Average Price: Inexpensive
Area: Porta Vittoria
Address: Via Baldassare Oltrocchi 11
20137 Milan Italy
Phone: 02 5511335

#103
Ida Del Castillo
Category: Women's Clothing
Average Price: Modest
Area: Centro Storico
Address: Corso Di Porta Ticinese
10520123 Milan Italy
Phone: 02 58112137

#104
Midali
Category: Women's Clothing
Average Price: Modest
Area: Porta Vittoria
Address: Via Lomellina 17
20133 Milan Italy
Phone: 02 70109955

#105
Kammi
Category: Shoe Stores
Average Price: Modest
Area: Città Studi
Address: Via Vallazze, 104
20131 Milan Italy
Phone: 02 70633041

#106
Gemelli
Category: Fashion
Average Price: Exclusive
Area: Parco Sempione, Washington
Address: Corso Vercelli, 16
20145 Milan Italy
Phone: 02 48000057

#107
Tally Weijl
Category: Women's Clothing
Average Price: Modest
Area: Stazione Centrale
Address: Corso Buenos Aires 41
20124 Milan Italy
Phone: 02 29527384

#108
L'altra Coco'
Category: Women's Clothing
Average Price: Expensive
Area: Centro Storico
Address: Viale Monte Nero, 7
20135 Milan Italy
Phone: 02 54101510

Milan Shopping Guide / The Most Recommended Stores in the City

#109
Orsetta Mantovani
Category: Women's Clothing
Average Price: Expensive
Area: Washington
Address: Corso Magenta 66
20100 Milan Italy
Phone: 02 36531856

#110
Metro
Category: Shopping Centers
Average Price: Modest
Area: Sesto San Giovanni
Address: Via Gozzano 19
20092 Cinisello Balsamo Italy
Phone: 02 617921

#111
Etro
Category: Outlet Stores, Men's Clothing, Women's Clothing
Average Price: Expensive
Area: Porta Vittoria
Address: Via Spartaco
320135 Milan Italy
Phone: 02 55020218

#112
Officina 171
Category: Women's Clothing, Men's Clothing
Average Price: Modest
Area: Città Studi
Address: Via Salieri
620131 Milan Italy
Phone: 02 2363722

#113
Rita Folli
Category: Women's Clothing
Average Price: Expensive
Area: Porta Romana
Address: Viale Bligny, 41
20136 Milan Italy
Phone: 02 58321193

#114
Missoni
Category: Art Galleries
Average Price: Modest
Area: Moscova
Address: Via Solferino
920121 Milan Italy
Phone: 02 80509604

#115
Paoletti
Category: Fashion
Average Price: Modest
Area: Centro Storico
Address: Piazza Sant' Eustorgio,
820122 Milan Italy
Phone: 02 58101218

#116
Rebus
Category: Home Decor, Gift Shops
Average Price: Modest
Area: Centro Storico
Address: Via Edmondo De Amicis
3520123 Milan Italy
Phone: 02 58106157

#117
Maria Grazia Tonolli
Category: Women's Clothing
Average Price: Modest
Area: Parco Sempione
Address: Piazza Virgilio 3
20123 Milan Italy
Phone: 02 4987002

#118
Cut
Category: Accessories
Average Price: Modest
Area: Centro Storico
Address: Corso Di Porta Ticinese, 58
20123 Milan Italy
Phone: 02 8394135

#119
Siddharta
Category: Arts & Crafts, Accessories, Women's Clothing
Average Price: Modest
Area: Porta Vittoria
Address: Corso XXII Marzo 40
20135 Milan Italy
Phone: 02 5456519

#120
Marina Nesta
Category: Women's Clothing
Average Price: Exclusive
Area: Centro Storico
Address: Via Dell'Orso 12
20121 Milan Italy
Phone: 02 878802

Milan Shopping Guide / The Most Recommended Stores in the City

---

#121
Atmosfera
Category: Men's Clothing, Women's Clothing
Average Price: Modest
Area: Città Studi
Address: Piazza Gobetti Pietro,
1220131 Milan Italy
Phone: 02 26683073

#122
Wait And See
Category: Women's Clothing
Average Price: Expensive
Area: Centro Storico
Address: Via Santa Marta 14
20123 Milan Italy
Phone: 02 72080195

#123
In's Mercato
Category: Convenience Stores,
Discount Store
Average Price: Modest
Area: Villa San Giovanni
Address: Via Privata Pindaro 3
20128 Milan Italy
Phone: 02 27005331

#124
Mortarotti
Category: Women's Clothing
Average Price: Expensive
Area: Fiera
Address: Via Belfiore 6
20121 Milan Italy
Phone: 02 48000021

#125
Blunauta
Category: Women's Clothing
Average Price: Expensive
Area: Centro Storico
Address: Via Dante 11
20123 Milan Italy
Phone: 02 86454266

#126
Turci Calzature
Category: Shoe Stores
Average Price: Expensive
Area: Porta Genova
Address: Piazzale Stazione Porta Genova
320144 Milan Italy
Phone: 02 58101658

#127
Coccinelle
Category: Leather Goods, Accessories
Average Price: Expensive
Area: Stazione Centrale
Address: Corso Buenos
Aires 4220124 Milan Italy
Phone: 02 20404755

#128
Trevisan & Co.
Category: Fashion
Average Price: Modest
Area: Centro Storico
Address: Corso Genova,
2020123 Milan Italy
Phone: 02 58100758

#129
Ipercoop
Category: Shopping Centers
Average Price: Modest
Area: Porta Vittoria
Address: Viale Umbria 4
20135 Milan Italy
Phone: 02 540451

#130
Baby2000 Donna
Category: Women's Clothing
Average Price: Modest
Area: Washington
Address: Via Dei Biancospini
20
20146 Milan Italy
Phone: 02 48951846

#131
Chiu Ting Sin
Category: Leather Goods
Average Price: Expensive
Area: Parco Sempione
Address: Via Paolo Sarpi, 19
20154 Milan Italy
Phone: 02 3315277

#132
Manee
Category: Shoe Stores
Average Price: Expensive
Area: Centro Storico
Address: Via Madonnina 10
20121 Milan Italy
Phone: 02 36590226

Milan Shopping Guide / The Most Recommended Stores in the City

---

#133
Cartoleria
Category: Toy Stores, Cards & Stationery
Average Price: Modest
Area: Garibaldi
Address: Viale Sondrio 2
20124 Milan Italy
Phone: 02 67072174

#134
Zara
Category: Women's Clothing, Men's Clothing
Average Price: Modest
Area: Certosa
Address: Via Grosotto 720149 Milan Italy
Phone: 02 3927178

#135
Manly
Category: Fashion
Average Price: Modest
Area: Centro Storico
Address: Via Gian Giacomo Mora
720123 Milan Italy
Phone: 02 45076245

#136
Beretti Officina Antiquaria
Category: Antiques, Used, Vintage & Consignment
Average Price: Expensive
Area: Parco Sempione
Address: Via Cesariano
820154 Milan Italy
Phone: 02 31055289

#137
House Of Cashmere
Category: Fashion
Average Price: Exclusive
Area: Palestro
Address: C. Buenos Aires,
220124 Milan Italy
Phone: 02 29405073

#138
Publishopping
Category: Outlet Stores
Average Price: Modest
Area: Garibaldi
Address: Via Boltraffio
1420159 Milan Italy
Phone: 02 89655541

#139
Hugo Boss
Category: Men's Clothing, Accessories
Average Price: Expensive
Area: Garibaldi
Address: Corso Giacomo
Matteotti 1120124 Milan Italy
Phone: 02 76394667

#140
La Piazzetta
Category: Women's Clothing
Average Price: Modest
Area: Porta Vittoria
Address: Corso Lodi
1320135 Milan Italy
Phone: 02 55199443

#141
Co.Import
Category: Home Decor
Average Price: Modest
Area: Bicocca
Address: Via Milanese,
1020099 Sesto San Giovanni Italy
Phone: 02 26264097

#142
Mercatino Dell'usato
Category: Antiques
Average Price: Inexpensive
Area: Cermenate
Address: Via Monti Sabini
920141 Milan Italy
Phone: 02 56816526

#143
Vittoria 1964
Category: Accessories
Average Price: Modest
Area: Fiera
Address: Via Michelangelo Buonarroti
1020145 Milan Italy
Phone: 02 43986861

#144
Ferrari E Balestra Pellicceria
Category: Women's Clothing
Average Price: Expensive
Area: Washington
Address: Via Valparaiso,
1020144 Milan Italy
Phone: 02 4987208

Milan Shopping Guide / The Most Recommended Stores in the City

#145
Place Minuit
Category: Women's Clothing,
Accessories, Shoe Stores
Average Price: Modest
Area: Moscova
Address: Corso Garibaldi 127
20121 Milan Italy
Phone: 02 36534181

#146
Nipper
Category: Art Galleries, Antiques
Average Price: Exclusive
Area: Porta Genova
Address: Ripa Di Porta Ticinese, 69
20143 Milan Italy
Phone: 338 9379578

#147
Atelier Gherardo Frassa
Category: Arts & Crafts, Home Decor
Average Price: Modest
Area: Porta Romana
Address: Via Tantardini 4
20136 Milan Italy
Phone: 02 55181750

#148
Tableware
Category: Outlet Stores, Home Decor
Average Price: Inexpensive
Area: Monumentale
Address: Via Piazzi 1
20159 Milan Italy
Phone: 02 66803897

#149
Share
Category: Used, Vintage & Consignment,
Women's Clothing, Children's Clothing
Average Price: Inexpensive
Area: Turro Gorla Greco
Address: Viale Padova 36
20131 Milan Italy
Phone: 02 39297800

#150
Lady Schapira
Category: Women's Clothing, Accessories
Average Price: Modest
Area: Centro Storico
Address: Corso Di Porta Vittoria
40020122 Milan Italy
Phone: 02 43129070

#151
Laboratorio Valentina
Category: Jewelry, Gift Shops
Average Price: Expensive
Area: Centro Storico
Address: Corso Di Porta Ticinese 69
20123 Milan Italy
Phone: 02 58104442

#152
Prada
Category: Leather Goods,
Men's Clothing, Shoe Stores
Average Price: Exclusive
Area: Centro Storico
Address: Galleria Vittorio Emanuele II 63
20121 Milan Italy
Phone: 02 876979

#153
Albert Calzature
Category: Shoe Stores
Average Price: Modest
Area: Città Studi
Address: Piazza Pietro Gobetti, 12
20131 Milan Italy
Phone: 02 2663957

#154
Marigo
Category: Women's Clothing
Average Price: Modest
Area: Centro Storico
Address: Corso Di Porta Romana 40
20122 Milan Italy
Phone: 02 58303112

#155
Oviesse
Category: Fashion, Cosmetics & Beauty
Supply, Home Decor
Average Price: Modest
Area: Cermenate
Address: Via Ripamonti 172
20141 Milan Italy
Phone: 02 57403091

#156
Preziosi Nel Tempo
Category: Jewelry
Average Price: Modest
Area: Città Studi
Address: Via Vallazze
11620131 Milan Italy
Phone: 02 23951730

Milan Shopping Guide / The Most Recommended Stores in the City

#157
Muji Italia
Category: Shopping Centers
Average Price: Modest
Area: Washington
Address: Corso Vercelli 11
20144 Milan Italy
Phone: 02 48517578

#158
To B
Category: Women's Clothing
Average Price: Modest
Area: Parco Sempione
Address: Via Vincenzo Monti, 27
20123 Milan Italy
Phone: 02 48024947

#159
Iliprandi
Category: Shoe Stores
Average Price: Modest
Area: Moscova
Address: Via Solferino, 11
20121 Milan Italy
Phone: 02 874723

#160
Cionti Outlet
Category: Outlet Stores
Average Price: Modest
Area: Porta Vittoria
Address: Via Cadore, 45
20135 Milan Italy
Phone: 02 89699628

#161
Gran Galà Di Creme
Category: Desserts, Patisserie/Cake Shop
Average Price: Inexpensive
Area: Turro Gorla Greco
Address: Via Emilio De Marchi 10
20125 Milan Italy
Phone: 02 66985638

#162
Spazio Verde Rame
Category: Art Supplies, Accessories
Average Price: Expensive
Area: Monumentale
Address: Via Mac Mahon 22
20155 Milan Italy
Phone: 02 49523890

#163
DB Living
Category: Accessories, Home Decor
Average Price: Modest
Area: Stazione Centrale
Address: Via Pisani 6
20100 Milan Italy
Phone: 02 36504189

#164
No30 Milano
Category: Women's Clothing
Average Price: Expensive
Area: Centro Storico
Address: Via Della Spiga, 30
20121 Milan Italy
Phone: 02 763172

#165
Tiger
Category: Office Equipment, Home Decor
Average Price: Inexpensive
Area: Parco Sempione, Centro Storico
Address: Piazzale Cadorna 4
20123 Milan Italy
Phone: 02 89092602

#166
Altromercato
Category: Grocery, Accessories
Average Price: Exclusive
Area: Porta Romana
Address: Corso San Gottardo 16
20136 Milan Italy
Phone: 02 83241498

#167
Borderline
Category: Fashion
Average Price: Modest
Area: Centro Storico
Address: Via Mora 12
20123 Milan Italy
Phone: 02 36511846

#168
Camiceria Lodi
Category: Fashion
Average Price: Modest
Area: Porta Vittoria
Address: C. Lodi, 15
20135 Milan Italy
Phone: 02 59901517

#169
Gio Gio Outlet
Category: Children's Clothing
Average Price: Inexpensive
Area: Stazione Centrale
Address: Via Giovanni Pier Luigi Da Palestrina 920124 Milan Italy
Phone: 02 66985571

#170
Ida Del Castillo Tessuti
Category: Fashion
Average Price: Modest
Area: Porta Genova
Address: Ripa Di Porta Ticinese, 10520143 Milan Italy
Phone: 02 58112137

#171
Milkroom
Category: Home Decor
Average Price: Modest
Area: Centro Storico
Address: Via De Amicis 59 20123 Milan Italy
Phone: 02 87238098

#172
L'Outlet Del Kasalingo
Category: Home & Garden, Outlet Stores
Average Price: Inexpensive
Area: Porta Vittoria, Porta Romana
Address: Corso Lodi 9320154 Milan Italy
Phone: 02 56814081

#173
Luna Stone
Category: Jewelry, Accessories
Average Price: Modest
Area: Washington
Address: Piazza De Angeli 1420146 Milan Italy
Phone: 02 39400762

#174
Manzoli
Category: Fashion
Average Price: Modest
Area: Fiera
Address: Via Traiano, 5020149 Milan Italy
Phone: 02 3271605

#175
Anonymous
Category: Women's Clothing
Average Price: Modest
Area: Centro Storico
Address: Via Edmondo De Amicis 720123 Milan Italy
Phone: 02 8392666

#176
Brian & Barry
Category: Fashion
Average Price: Modest
Area: Washington
Address: Corso Vercelli, 2320144 Milan Italy
Phone: 02 86463562

#177
Mariza Tassy
Category: Women's Clothing
Average Price: Expensive
Area: Centro Storico
Address: Via Molino Delle Armi 4520123 Milan Italy
Phone: 02 89415364

#178
La Voglia
Category: Fashion
Average Price: Modest
Area: Washington
Address: C. Vercelli, 2520144 Milan Italy
Phone: 02 48013246

#179
Andrea Canevelli
Category: Fashion
Average Price: Exclusive
Area: Parco Sempione
Address: Via Abbondio Sangiorgio, 620145 Milan Italy
Phone: 02 34538657

#180
Verger
Category: Fashion, Cafes
Average Price: Expensive
Area: Moscova
Address: Via Varese 120121 Milan Italy
Phone: 02 86998276

Milan Shopping Guide / The Most Recommended Stores in the City

---

#181
Cappelleria Melegari
Category: Accessories
Average Price: Expensive
Area: Parco Sempione
Address: Via Paolo Sarpi,
1920154 Milan Italy
Phone: 02 312094

#182
Menoni
Category: Jewelry
Average Price: Modest
Area: Porta Genova
Address: Via La Spezia, 1120142 Milan Italy
Phone: 02 8958971

#183
Hangarbicocca
Category: Art Galleries, Museums
Average Price: Modest
Area: Bicocca
Address: Via Chiese 220126 Milan Italy
Phone: 02 66111573

#184
Mentine Milano
Category: Home Decor, Used, Vintage & Consignment
Average Price: Expensive
Area: Porta Genova
Address: Ripa Di Porta Ticinese, 39
20143 Milan Italy
Phone: 02 89404441

#185
Cos
Category: Men's Clothing, Women's Clothing
Average Price: Modest
Area: Centro Storico
Address: Corso Venezia 5
20121 Milan Italy
Phone: 02 76280649

#186
Martin Luciano E Figli
Category: Fabric Stores, Used, Vintage & Consignment
Average Price: Modest
Area: Porta Genova
Address: Alzaia Naviglio Grande 58
20144 Milan Italy
Phone: 02 58101173

#187
O Bag
Category: Accessories
Average Price: Modest
Area: Palestro
Address: Via Melzo
3620129 Milan Italy
Phone: 02 29534580

#188
Casile & Casile
Category: Women's Clothing, Men's Clothing
Average Price: Expensive
Area: Porta Genova
Address: Via Tortona 920144 Milan Italy
Phone: 02 466299

#189
Les Chaussures Mon Amour
Category: Shoe Stores
Average Price: Expensive
Area: Centro Storico
Address: Corso Di Porta Ticinese N.
10320123 Milan Italy
Phone: 02 83241620

#190
H&M
Category: Men's Clothing, Women's Clothing
Average Price: Modest
Area: Certosa
Address: Via Traiano 74
20149 Milan Italy
Phone: 02 39260016

#191
Tiger
Category: Discount Store, Gift Shops, Home Decor
Average Price: Inexpensive
Area: Centro Storico
Address: Via Nerino 12
20123 Milan Italy
Phone: 02 87075150

#192
Upim
Category: Shopping Centers
Average Price: Modest
Area: Garibaldi
Address: Via Carlo Farini 79
20159 Milan Italy
Phone: 02 680148

Milan Shopping Guide / The Most Recommended Stores in the City

#193
Barbour Store
Category: Fashion
Average Price: Exclusive
Area: Centro Storico
Address: Via Edmondo De Amicis, 24
20123 Milan Italy
Phone: 02 58109012

#194
OVS
Category: Department Stores
Average Price: Modest
Area: Washington
Address: Via Redaelli 2/A
20146 Milan Italy
Phone: 02 489588218

#195
Carrena
Category: Men's Clothing, Women's Clothing
Average Price: Expensive
Area: Washington
Address: Via Giorgio Washington, 88
20146 Milan Italy
Phone: 02 471333

#196
Cotton Factory Outlet
Category: Outlet Stores
Average Price: Modest
Area: Porta Vittoria
Address: Viale Umbria 3
20135 Milan Italy
Phone: 02 54071623

#197
Pracchi Discount
Category: Shopping Centers, Grocery
Average Price: Modest
Area: Porta Vittoria
Address: Via Simone D'orsenigo,
920135 Milan Italy
Phone: 02 55192345

#198
Clerici
Category: Hobby Shops
Average Price: Inexpensive
Area: Cermenate
Address: Via De Sanctis,
3320100 Milan Italy
Phone: 02 8467739

#199
Buba International Designer
Category: Fashion
Average Price: Expensive
Area: Palestro
Address: Via Spallanzani 6
20129 Milan Italy
Phone: 02 29409634

#200
Nadine
Category: Women's Clothing
Average Price: Modest
Area: Centro Storico
Address: Via Dante 16
20121 Milan Italy
Phone: 02 86915906

#201
Pinko
Category: Women's Clothing
Average Price: Expensive
Area: Moscova
Address: Corso Como 11
20154 Milan Italy
Phone: 02 63470389

#202
Jean Marie
Category: Women's Clothing
Average Price: Modest
Area: Washington
Address: Piazza De Angeli 14
20149 Milan Italy
Phone: 02 4043980

#203
Fatto A Mano
Category: Women's Clothing
Average Price: Expensive
Area: Washington
Address: Via San Michele Del
Carso, 620144 Milan Italy
Phone: 02 48517744

#204
Kristina Ti
Category: Women's Clothing
Average Price: Expensive
Area: Moscova
Address: Via Solferino,
1820121 Milan Italy
Phone: 02 653379

Milan Shopping Guide / The Most Recommended Stores in the City

---

#205
Vale
Category: Women's Clothing
Average Price: Expensive
Area: Fiera
Address: Via Marcantonio Colonna, 14
20149 Milan Italy
Phone: 02 33100204

#206
10 Corso Como
Category: Art Galleries
Average Price: Exclusive
Area: Moscova
Address: Corso Como
1020154 Milan Italy
Phone: 02 29013581

#207
Mango
Category: Accessories, Women's Clothing
Average Price: Modest
Area: Stazione Centrale
Address: Corso Buenos Aires
2320124 Milan Italy
Phone: 02 20241915

#208
Blue Deep
Category: Women's Clothing
Average Price: Modest
Area: Moscova
Address: Via Solferino
520121 Milan Italy
Phone: 02 876702

#209
Salvatore+Marie
Category: Fashion
Average Price: Modest
Area: Porta Genova
Address: Via Vigevano
3320144 Milan Italy
Phone: 02 89422152

#210
Harold'S Boutique
Category: Women's Clothing
Average Price: Expensive
Area: Washington
Address: Via Vincenzo Foppa,
2520144 Milan Italy
Phone: 02 4693156

#211
OVS
Category: Men's Clothing, Women's Clothing
Average Price: Modest
Area: Centro Storico
Address: Via Spadari 2
20123 Milan Italy
Phone: 02 89010750

#212
Carrè
Category: Antiques, Furniture Stores
Average Price: Exclusive
Area: Washington
Address: Viale Papiniano
3820123 Milan Italy
Phone: 02 468189

#213
Pour Amour
Category: Women's Clothing, Accessories
Average Price: Modest
Area: Washington
Address: Via Cimarosa 3/A Angolo Corso
Vercelli 20100 Milan Italy
Phone: 02 49518184

#214
Ennji
Category: Accessories, Women's Clothing
Average Price: Modest
Area: Porta Genova
Address: Corso Colombo
720144 Milan Italy
Phone: 02 58109783

#215
Bruno Bordese
Category: Shoe Stores
Average Price: Modest
Area: Moscova
Address: Via Maroncelli,
220154 Milan Italy
Phone: 02 63793659

#216
Save My Bag
Category: Luggage, Accessories
Average Price: Modest
Area: Centro Storico
Address: Via Alessandro Manzoni
3720121 Milan Italy
Phone: 02 62694947

#217
Brandy Melville
Category: Fashion
Average Price: Modest
Area: Moscova
Address: Via Statuto, 16
20121 Milan Italy
Phone: 02 29004294

#218
La Bottega Coquelicot
Category: Women's Clothing
Average Price: Modest
Area: Centro Storico
Address: Viale Montenero 25
20135 Milan Italy
Phone: 02 54106014

#219
Cenerentola
Category: Shoe Stores
Average Price: Modest
Area: Bande Nere, Fiera
Address: Via Rembrandt 44
20148 Milan Italy
Phone: 02 87036815

#220
Les Chaussures Mon Amour
Category: Shoe Stores
Average Price: Expensive
Area: Fiera
Address: Via Cherubini 3
20145 Milan Italy
Phone: 02 48000535

#221
Maglificio R. Scaglione
Category: Women's Clothing
Average Price: Expensive
Area: Centro Storico
Address: Via SAN Vincenzo, 1
20123 Milan Italy
Phone: 02 89403751

#222
Après-Midi
Category: Accessories
Average Price: Modest
Area: Garibaldi
Address: Via Pastrengo, 7
20159 Milan Italy
Phone: 02 6889534

#223
Vertigini
Category: Shoe Stores, Accessories
Average Price: Inexpensive
Area: Porta Vittoria
Address: Viale Umbria 7
20135 Milan Italy
Phone: 02 91637579

#224
Rossella Carrara
Category: Women's Clothing
Average Price: Expensive
Area: Centro Storico
Address: Via Torino, 51
20123 Milan Italy
Phone: 02 80506594

#225
Grand Market
Category: Department Stores
Average Price: Inexpensive
Area: Porta Romana
Address: Viale Sabotino 16
20135 Milan Italy
Phone: 02 58315033

#226
Pull & Bear
Category: Men's Clothing
Average Price: Modest
Area: Centro Storico
Address: Via Torino 22
20123 Milan Italy
Phone: 02 89014122

#227
ADV Deal
Category: Outlet Stores
Average Price: Modest
Area: Porta Vittoria
Address: Via Nervesa 12
20139 Milan Italy
Phone: 02 89767409

#228
Puma Store
Category: Shoe Stores
Average Price: Modest
Area: Stazione Centrale
Address: Via Casati 1A
20124 Milan Italy
Phone: 02 29408661

Milan Shopping Guide / The Most Recommended Stores in the City

#229
Crisci
Category: Fashion
Average Price: Modest
Area: Porta Vittoria
Address: Corso Ventidue Marzo, 8
20135 Milan Italy
Phone: 02 59901113

#230
A&C Ghepard
Category: Outlet Stores
Average Price: Modest
Area: Porta Romana
Address: Via Marco d'Agrate 41
20139 Milan Italy
Phone: 02 57401040

#231
Jeos
Category: Shoe Stores
Average Price: Modest
Area: Porta Vittoria
Address: Viale Corsica 39
20133 Milan Italy
Phone: 02 70104896

#232
Zori
Category: Accessories
Average Price: Modest
Area: Porta Romana
Address: Via Crema 8
20135 Milan Italy
Phone: 02 89072765

#233
Miki Thumb Boutique
Category: Women's Clothing
Average Price: Expensive
Area: Centro Storico
Address: Via San Giovanni Sul Muro, 12
20121 Milan Italy
Phone: 02 36520473

#234
Giorgio IV Outlet
Category: Fashion
Average Price: Modest
Area: Porta Vittoria
Address: Via Lomellina
2520133 Milan Italy
Phone: 02 70120980

#235
Melina Mannino
Category: Sewing & Alterations,
Women's Clothing
Average Price: Modest
Area: Porta Genova
Address: Via Tortona 4
20144 Milan Italy
Phone: 02 89422044

#236
Gianni Versace
Category: Men's Clothing, Women's Clothing
Average Price: Exclusive
Area: Centro Storico
Address: Via Monte Napoleone 11
20121 Milan Italy
Phone: 02 76008528

#237
Arredamenti Mangione
Category: Outlet Stores
Average Price: Expensive
Area: Bovisa
Address: Via Andreoli 2020158 Milan Italy
Phone: 02 3760653

#238
Camiceria Vitali
Category: Men's Clothing
Average Price: Modest
Area: Porta Romana
Address: Corso San Gottardo 7
20136 Milan Italy
Phone: 02 58111991

#239
Pilatno
Category: Fashion
Average Price: Modest
Area: Turro Gorla Greco
Address: Via Agordat 15
20127 Milan Italy
Phone: 02 2613337

#240
Dada
Category: Women's Clothing
Average Price: Modest
Area: Porta Genova
Address: Corso Colombo
Cristoforo 620144 Milan Italy
Phone: 02 83241709

Milan Shopping Guide / The Most Recommended Stores in the City

#241
Larusmiani Outlet
Category: Outlet Stores
Average Price: Modest
Area: Monumentale
Address: Via Ulderico Ollearo, 8
20155 Milan Italy
Phone: 02 33002600

#242
Guendj
Category: Used, Vintage & Consignment
Average Price: Modest
Area: Porta Genova
Address: Ripa Porta Ticinese 47
20144 Milan Italy
Phone: 02 58101492

#243
Dama Creazione
Category: Jewelry
Average Price: Modest
Area: Porta Vittoria
Address: Corso XXII Marzo 57
20129 Milan Italy
Phone: 02 39666439

#244
Elle Creat
Category: Women's Clothing
Average Price: Modest
Area: Porta Vittoria
Address: Viale Premuda,
2020129 Milan Italy
Phone: 02 76002510

#245
Midali
Category: Women's Clothing
Average Price: Modest
Area: Porta Vittoria
Address: Via Fratelli Bronzetti 23
20129 Milan Italy
Phone: 02 70005514

#246
Outlet Niki
Category: Outlet Stores
Average Price: Modest
Area: Porta Vittoria, Centro Storico
Address: Viale Montenero, 78
20135 Milan Italy
Phone: 02 5468855

#247
Sartoria Bassani
Category: Fashion, Sewing & Alterations
Average Price: Modest
Area: Centro Storico
Address: Via Cesare Correnti, 11
20123 Milan Italy
Phone: 02 89420404

#248
Milan Mega Store
Category: Sports Wear
Average Price: Expensive
Area: Centro Storico
Address: Corso Vittorio Emanuele II
20122 Milan Italy
Phone: 02 49580176

#249
Marco
Category: Shoe Stores
Average Price: Expensive
Area: Centro Storico
Address: Via Torino 27
20123 Milan Italy
Phone: 02 86460411

#250
Quel Che C'è
Category: Discount Store
Average Price: Modest
Area: Porta Romana
Address: Via Orobia
1120139 Milan Italy
Phone: 02 56816202

#251
Elia
Category: Men's Clothing
Average Price: Modest
Area: Fiera
Address: Piazza Riccardo Wagner 1
20145 Milan Italy
Phone: 02 4986804

#252
Il Tirolo A Milano
Category: Fashion, Specialty Food
Average Price: Exclusive
Area: Porta Genova
Address: Viale Coni Zugna 62
20144 Milan Italy
Phone: 02 8373841

Milan Shopping Guide / The Most Recommended Stores in the City

#253
Antonioli
Category: Men's Clothing, Women's Clothing
Average Price: Exclusive
Area: Porta Genova
Address: Via Pasquale Paoli 1
20143 Milan Italy
Phone: 02 36566494

#254
Gazzetta Store
Category: Outlet Stores
Average Price: Modest
Area: Centro Storico
Address: Galleria San Carlo
20122 Milan Italy
Phone: 02 76280654

#255
Design Supermarket
Category: Home Decor
Average Price: Modest
Area: Centro Storico
Address: Via Santa Radegonda 3
20121 Milan Italy
Phone: 02 88521

#256
Stiù Shoes
Category: Shoe Stores
Average Price: Expensive
Area: Centro Storico
Address: Corso Di Porta Ticinese, 105
20123 Milan Italy
Phone: 02 8322020

#257
Emmegross
Category: Lingerie, Outlet Stores
Average Price: Modest
Area: Bovisa
Address: Via Carnevali 116
20158 Milan Italy
Phone: 02 39317864

#258
Il Cameo
Category: Women's Clothing, Accessories
Average Price: Modest
Area: Centro Storico
Address: Via San Carpoforo, 6
20121 Milan Italy
Phone: 349 2448263

#259
La Zacca
Category: Accessories, Arts & Crafts
Average Price: Inexpensive
Area: Centro Storico
Address: Via San Carpoforo 2
20121 Milan Italy
Phone: 02 45486886

#260
Gucci
Category: Children's Clothing, Men's Clothing, Women's Clothing
Average Price: Expensive
Area: Centro Storico
Address: Via Monte Napoleone 5
20121 Milan Italy
Phone: 02 771271

#261
Diffusione Tessile
Category: Women's Clothing
Average Price: Modest
Area: Centro Storico
Address: Galleria San Carlo 6
20122 Milan Italy
Phone: 02 76000829

#262
The Store
Category: Shoe Stores, Men's Clothing
Average Price: Modest
Area: Moscova
Address: Via Solferino 720121 Milan Italy
Phone: 02 874723

#263
Ago E Spago
Category: Shoe Stores
Average Price: Modest
Area: Porta Romana
Address: Viale Col Di Lana 12
20136 Milan Italy
Phone: 02 8357122

#264
Zara HOME
Category: Home Decor
Average Price: Modest
Area: Washington
Address: Corso Vercelli 37
20144 Milan Italy
Phone: 8009 05685

Milan Shopping Guide / The Most Recommended Stores in the City

---

#265
Suede
Category: Luggage, Women's Clothing
Average Price: Expensive
Area: Centro Storico
Address: Via Cesare Correnti 21
20123 Milan Italy
Phone: 02 83200592

#266
Shopping Lifts Spirit
Category: Fashion
Average Price: Exclusive
Area: Moscova
Address: Via Maroncelli, 3
20154 Milan Italy
Phone: 02 29063125

#267
Elle Zeta
Category: Outlet Stores
Average Price: Modest
Area: Bovisa
Address: Via Angelo Brofferio 10
20158 Milan Italy
Phone: 02 39321377

#268
Green Apple
Category: Watches, Accessories
Average Price: Modest
Area: Porta Genova
Address: Via Vigevano 11
20144 Milan Italy
Phone: 02 83390116

#269
Berluti
Category: Shoe Stores, Accessories
Average Price: Modest
Area: Centro Storico
Address: Via Sant'Andrea 16
20121 Milan Italy
Phone: 02 77877011

#270
Indumenti Da Lavoro E Sport
Category: Fashion
Average Price: Modest
Area: Garibaldi
Address: Via Carlo Farini,
5820159 Milan Italy
Phone: 02 66800975

#271
Camper
Category: Shoe Stores
Average Price: Modest
Area: Porta Romana
Address: Porta Ticinese 59
20136 Milan Italy
Phone: 02 58103844

#272
MAX & Co.
Category: Women's Clothing
Average Price: Modest
Area: Porta Vittoria
Address: Corso Xxii Marzo
2020135 Milan Italy
Phone: 02 5450821

#273
P.A.S.T.I.C.C.E.R.I.A
Category: Fashion
Average Price: Modest
Area: Parco Sempione
Address: Via Vincenzo Monti, 28
20145 Milan Italy
Phone: 02 4818218

#274
H & M
Category: Men's Clothing, Women's Clothing
Average Price: Modest
Area: Stazione Centrale
Address: Corso Buenos Aires 56
20124 Milan Italy
Phone: 02 20240171

#275
Yubiz
Category: Women's Clothing
Average Price: Expensive
Area: Porta Vittoria
Address: Corso Lodi, 9
20135 Milan Italy
Phone: 02 54116547

#276
True Religion Brand Jeans Italy
Category: Fashion
Average Price: Modest
Area: Porta Genova
Address: Via Morimondo, 5
20143 Milan Italy
Phone: 02 8135202

Milan Shopping Guide / The Most Recommended Stores in the City

---

#277
Brera
Category: Art Galleries
Average Price: Modest
Area: Centro Storico
Address: Via Fiori Chiari
2020121 Milan Italy
Phone: 02 80502733

#278
Luna Orientale
Category: Women's Clothing
Average Price: Modest
Area: Washington
Address: Via Rembrandt 9
20147 Milan Italy
Phone: 02 338478200

#279
Nuvola
Category: Women's Clothing
Average Price: Modest
Area: Monumentale
Address: Via Piero Della Francesca, 10
20154 Milan Italy
Phone: 02 341860

#280
Silvia
Category: Leather Goods, Shoe Stores
Average Price: Expensive
Area: Centro Storico
Address: Corso Di Porta Ticinese
1620123 Milan Italy
Phone: 02 89404200

#281
Boutique Luana
Category: Women's Clothing
Average Price: Modest
Area: Città Studi
Address: Via Giovanni Pacini 8
20131 Milan Italy
Phone: 02 2360562

#282
Cagi Maglierie
Category: Men's Clothing, Outlet Stores
Average Price: Modest
Area: Porta Genova
Address: Viale Cassala 46
20143 Milan Italy
Phone: 02 58101283

#283
In + Out By Emme Stile
Category: Women's Clothing
Average Price: Modest
Area: Fiera
Address: Via Correggio 7520149 Milan Italy
Phone: 02 4816617

#284
Prosio
Category: Shoe Stores
Average Price: Modest
Area: Porta Vittoria
Address: Corso Xxii Marzo, 5
20129 Milan Italy
Phone: 02 55180122

#285
Scarpe & Scarpe
Category: Shoe Stores
Average Price: Modest
Area: Washington
Address: Via Redaelli Pietro,
220146 Milan Italy
Phone: 02 42291056

#286
Lollipops
Category: Fashion
Average Price: Modest
Area: Cologno Monzese
Address: Via Indipendenza
20093 Cologno Monzese Italy
Phone: 02 27307557

#287
Silvia Scordia
Category: Jewelry
Average Price: Expensive
Area: Porta Romana
Address: Via Sabotino 12
20135 Milan Italy
Phone: 02 89655707

#288
Colorificio Candiani
Category: Home Decor
Average Price: Modest
Area: Bovisa
Address: Via Candiani Giuseppe
13020158 Milan Italy
Phone: 02 3760102

#289
Beautiful House
Category: Home Decor
Average Price: Modest
Area: Porta Vittoria, Centro Storico
Address: Viale Monte Nero 14
20135 Milan Italy
Phone: 02 5468349

#290
P.A.R.O.S.H.
Category: Women's Clothing
Average Price: Modest
Area: Moscova
Address: Corso Di Porta Nuova 46
20121 Milan Italy
Phone: 02 29003559

#291
Sarpi Conf
Category: Men's Clothing
Average Price: Modest
Area: Parco Sempione
Address: Via Paolo Sarpi, 61
20154 Milan Italy
Phone: 02 33603395

#292
La Scialuppa
Category: Fashion
Average Price: Modest
Area: Porta Vittoria
Address: Via Macedonio Melloni 75
20129 Milan Italy
Phone: 02 717239

#293
L'artiglio
Category: Home Decor
Average Price: Modest
Area: Porta Genova
Address: Alzaia Naviglio Grande 108
20144 Milan Italy
Phone: 02 58108719

#294
Kammi
Category: Shoe Stores
Average Price: Modest
Area: Città Studi
Address: Via Vallazze 104
20131 Milan Italy
Phone: 02 70633041

#295
Al Barza
Category: Men's Clothing
Average Price: Modest
Area: Parco Sempione
Address: Via Antonio Scarpa 9
20145 Milan Italy
Phone: 2433 470

#296
Marella
Category: Women's Clothing
Average Price: Expensive
Area: Porta Vittoria
Address: Corso XXII Marzo 4
20135 Milan Italy
Phone: 02 5463754

#297
H&M
Category: Men's Clothing, Women's Clothing
Average Price: Inexpensive
Area: Stazione Centrale
Address: Corso Buenos Aires 75
20124 Milan Italy
Phone: 02 6782161

#298
And Camicie
Category: Women's Clothing, Men's Clothing
Average Price: Modest
Area: Centro Storico
Address: Via Cavin Di Sala 388
20122 Milan Italy
Phone: 041 5709211

#299
Antonia
Category: Accessories, Women's Clothing
Average Price: Modest
Area: Centro Storico
Address: Via Cusani 5
20121 Milan Italy
Phone: 02 86998340

#300
Muji
Category: Fashion
Average Price: Expensive
Area: Centro Storico
Address: Via Torino 51
20123 Milan Italy
Phone: 02 809441

Milan Shopping Guide / The Most Recommended Stores in the City

#301
Tiger
Category: Gift Shops, Home Decor, Office Equipment
Average Price: Inexpensive
Area: Stazione Centrale
Address: Corso Buenos Aires 69
20131 Milan Italy
Phone: 02 29537465

#302
Jamin Puech
Category: Accessories
Average Price: Expensive
Area: Moscova
Address: Via Solferino 3
20121 Milan Italy
Phone: 02 92870584

#303
O Bag
Category: Accessories, Luggage
Average Price: Modest
Area: Porta Genova
Address: Via Tortona 12
20144 Milan Italy
Phone: 02 89409722

#304
Tappezzerie In Stoffa Casiraghi
Category: Home Decor
Average Price: Modest
Area: Certosa
Address: Via Nuvolone Panfilo 27
20156 Milan Italy
Phone: 02 38000169

#305
Rame Ceramiche d'Arte
Category: Arts & Crafts, Gift Shops
Average Price: Modest
Area: Centro Storico
Address: Via Francesco Sforza 46
20122 Milan Italy
Phone: 02 58307498

#306
Tezenis
Category: Lingerie, Women's Clothing
Average Price: Modest
Area: Certosa
Address: Via Grossotto
920149 Milan Italy
Phone: 02 33007353

#307
Amon
Category: Fashion
Average Price: Modest
Area: Centro Storico
Address: Corso Genova, 13
20123 Milan Italy
Phone: 02 89400062

#308
Fratelli Rossetti
Category: Shoe Stores
Average Price: Exclusive
Area: Centro Storico
Address: Via Montenapoleone 1
20121 Milan Italy
Phone: 02 76021650

#309
Benetton
Category: Men's Clothing, Women's Clothing, Children's Clothing
Average Price: Modest
Area: Parco Sempione
Address: Corso Vercelli 8
20145 Milan Italy
Phone: 02 43351121

#310
100 Montaditos
Category: Tapas Bars, Shopping Centers
Average Price: Modest
Area: Sesto San Giovanni
Address: Via Milanese
20099 Sesto San Giovanni Italy
Phone: 02 2412431

#311
Cavalli E Nastri
Category: Women's Clothing
Average Price: Expensive
Area: Centro Storico
Address: Via Gian Giacomo Mora
320123 Milan Italy
Phone: 02 89409052

#312
Prada
Category: Shoe Stores, Accessories
Average Price: Exclusive
Area: Centro Storico
Address: C. Venezia,
320121 Milan Italy
Phone: 02 76001842

Milan Shopping Guide / The Most Recommended Stores in the City

---

#313
Adriana Galli
Category: Jewelry, Accessories
Average Price: Expensive
Area: Fiera
Address: Via Capponi Pier Luigi 2
20145 Milan Italy
Phone: 02 89070536

#314
Glamour In Rose
Category: Accessories, Shoe Stores, Women's Clothing
Average Price: Expensive
Area: Moscova
Address: Via Solferino 12
20121 Milan Italy
Phone: 02 653822

#315
Au Nom De La Rose
Category: Florists, Gift Shops
Average Price: Expensive
Area: Fiera
Address: Piazza Wagner Riccardo
120145 Milan Italy
Phone: 02 48009254

#316
Baby Boom
Category: Thrift Stores
Average Price: Modest
Area: Porta Genova
Address: Via Savona 2A
20144 Milan Italy
Phone: 02 58110347

#317
Gaffuri Virginio
Category: Fashion
Average Price: Modest
Area: Affori
Address: Viale Affori, 1
20161 Milan Italy
Phone: 02 66220482

#318
D-Magazine Outlet
Category: Women's Clothing
Average Price: Expensive
Area: Centro Storico
Address: Via Alessandro Manzoni
4420121 Milan Italy
Phone: 02 36514365

#319
Model Moda
Category: Leather Goods
Average Price: Modest
Area: Centro Storico
Address: Cso Porta Romana, 52
20122 Milan Italy
Phone: 02 58303160

#320
Vanità
Category: Jewelry, Tattoo, Piercing
Average Price: Modest
Area: Porta Genova
Address: Via Vigevano 45
20144 Milan Italy
Phone: 02 8372692

#321
Le Jardin Et La Campagne
Category: Interior Design, Home Decor
Average Price: Modest
Area: Parco Sempione
Address: Largo V Alpini 7
20145 Milan Italy
Phone: 02 4699138

#322
Nucci
Category: Fashion
Average Price: Modest
Area: Corsica, Porta Vittoria
Address: Via Lomellina, 56
20133 Milan Italy
Phone: 02 70126680

#323
Les Indiennes Texstyles
Category: Fashion
Average Price: Modest
Area: Centro Storico
Address: Via Ausonio 7
20123 Milan Italy
Phone: 02 45497563

#324
Liu Jo
Category: Women's Clothing, Accessories
Average Price: Modest
Area: Stazione Centrale
Address: Piazza Duca D'Aosta
120125 Milan Italy
Phone: 02 66989218

Milan Shopping Guide / The Most Recommended Stores in the City

#325
Pause
Category: Bars, Women's Clothing
Average Price: Modest
Area: Buenos Aires
Address: Via Federico Ozanam 7
20129 Milan Italy
Phone: 02 39528151

#326
Roberto Leon
Category: Fashion
Average Price: Expensive
Area: Porta Vittoria
Address: Corso XXII Marzo 39
20129 Milan Italy
Phone: 02 7384844

#327
Siste's
Category: Women's Clothing
Average Price: Modest
Area: Palestro
Address: Corso Buenos Aires
20124 Milan Italy
Phone: 02 20400337

#328
Zeta Calzature
Category: Shoe Stores
Average Price: Exclusive
Area: Centro Storico
Address: Corso Genova, 4
20123 Milan Italy
Phone: 02 58101823

#329
Arpaia Francesco
Category: Jewelry
Average Price: Modest
Area: Porta Genova
Address: Via Argelati Filippo, 220143 Milan Italy
Phone: 02 89403862

#330
Coccinella
Category: Fashion
Average Price: Modest
Area: Porta Vittoria
Address: Via Francesco Anzani, 2
20135 Milan Italy
Phone: 02 55196386

#331
Dressebook
Category: Bookstores, Used, Vintage & Consignment, Accessories
Average Price: Modest
Area: Porta Vittoria
Address: Via Lomellina 9
20133 Milan Italy
Phone: 02 36526752

#332
Nadine
Category: Women's Clothing
Average Price: Modest
Area: Parco Sempione
Address: Corso Vercelli 8
20145 Milan Italy
Phone: 02 43510306

#333
Coccinelle Store
Category: Accessories
Average Price: Modest
Area: Centro Storico
Address: Via Bigli 28
20121 Milan Italy
Phone: 02 76028161

#334
Carhartt
Category: Fashion
Average Price: Modest
Area: Centro Storico
Address: Corso Di Porta Ticinese N.103
20123 Milan Italy
Phone: 02 89421932

#335
Ferrari Store
Category: Men's Clothing, Women's Clothing
Average Price: Expensive
Area: Centro Storico
Address: Via Berchet 2
20121 Milan Italy
Phone: 02 49490815

#336
Alice
Category: Children's Clothing
Average Price: Modest
Area: Corsica, Porta Vittoria
Address: Via Lomellina 5220133 Milan Italy
Phone: 02 743412

Milan Shopping Guide / The Most Recommended Stores in the City

---

#337
Lo Showroom
Category: Women's Clothing, Accessories
Average Price: Modest
Area: Porta Genova
Address: Ripa Di Porta Ticinese 57
20143 Milan Italy
Phone: 02 83660749

#338
One Brera
Category: Women's Clothing
Average Price: Modest
Area: Centro Storico
Address: Via Brera 29
20121 Milan Italy
Phone: 02 866182

#339
L'Atelier Di Simongia
Category: Fashion
Average Price: Modest
Area: Porta Genova
Address: Via Savona 94/A
20144 Milan Italy
Phone: 338 7252453

#340
Non Solo Vintage
Category: Accessories, Women's Clothing
Average Price: Expensive
Area: Garibaldi
Address: Via Pietro Borsieri 32
20159 Milan Italy
Phone: 02 6886601

#341
Banana Republic
Category: Men's Clothing, Women's Clothing
Average Price: Expensive
Area: Centro Storico
Address: Corso Vittorio Emanuele II 24
20122 Milan Italy
Phone: 02 303529

#342
Muji
Category: Office Equipment, Home Decor
Average Price: Expensive
Area: Buenos Aires
Address: Corso Buenos Aires
3620124 Milan Italy
Phone: 02 74281169

#343
Cavalli E Nastri
Category: Used, Vintage & Consignment
Average Price: Expensive
Area: Centro Storico
Address: Via Brera, 2
20121 Milan Italy
Phone: 02 72000449

#344
Scarpe & Scarpe
Category: Shopping Centers
Average Price: Modest
Area: Porta Romana
Address: Corso San Gottardo 39
20136 Milan Italy
Phone: 02 58104122

#345
Montezemolo
Category: Fashion
Average Price: Expensive
Area: Centro Storico
Address: Corso Genova, 24
20123 Milan Italy
Phone: 02 29000184

#346
Oscar
Category: Accessories
Average Price: Modest
Area: Parco Sempione
Address: Via Paolo Sarpi, 15
20154 Milan Italy
Phone: 02 36555951

#347
Guglielminotti
Category: Fashion
Average Price: Modest
Area: Centro Storico
Address: Corso Genova 15
20123 Milan Italy
Phone: 02 89402439

#348
Valigeria Moderna
Category: Accessories
Average Price: Modest
Area: Porta Vittoria
Address: Corso XXII Marzo 24
20135 Milan Italy
Phone: 02 55195439

Milan Shopping Guide / The Most Recommended Stores in the City

---

#349
Toys Center
Category: Toy Stores
Average Price: Modest
Area: Cermenate
Address: Via Antonini
3220141 Milan Italy
Phone: 02 87281241

#350
Boutique Pucci
Category: Fashion
Average Price: Modest
Area: Washington
Address: Via Solari Angolo Piazza Del
Rosario 20144 Milan Italy
Phone: 02 8360390

#351
Isola Della Moda
Category: Women's Clothing
Average Price: Modest
Area: Garibaldi
Address: Via Carmagnola, 7
20159 Milan Italy
Phone: 02 87390245

#352
Elizabeth The First
Category: Fashion
Average Price: Modest
Area: Porta Genova
Address: Alzaia Naviglio Grande, 44
20144 Milan Italy
Phone: 02 89077927

#353
Jack & Jones
Category: Men's Clothing, Women's Clothing
Average Price: Modest
Area: Cinisello Balsamo
Address: Via Panfilo Castaldi 15
20092 Cinisello Balsamo Italy
Phone: 02 61291089

#354
Opportunity Shop
Category: Thrift Stores
Average Price: Inexpensive
Area: Monumentale
Address: Viale Jenner 12A
20159 Milan Italy
Phone: 02 87396623

#355
PUMA Outlet
Category: Shoe Stores, Men's Clothing,
Women's Clothing
Average Price: Modest
Area: Porta Vittoria
Address: Viale Montenero
2220135 Milan Italy
Phone: 2599 02227

#356
I Love Shopping
Category: Women's Clothing
Average Price: Modest
Area: Sesto San Giovanni
Address: Via Cesare Da Sesto 134
20099 Sesto San Giovanni Italy
Phone: 02 24309860

#357
La Factory Milano
Category: Fashion
Average Price: Modest
Area: Palestro
Address: Viale Vittorio Veneto
2020124 Milan Italy
Phone: 02 39663286

#358
Bershka
Category: Women's Clothing, Men's Clothing
Average Price: Expensive
Area: Centro Storico
Address: Corso Vittorio Emanuele II 22
20122 Milan Italy
Phone: 02 76394975

#359
Nano Bleu
Category: Toy Stores, Gift Shops
Average Price: Inexpensive
Area: Centro Storico
Address: Corso Vittorio Emanuele II
1520122 Milan Italy
Phone: 02 76020595

#360
Eleonora Shoes
Category: Shoe Stores
Average Price: Modest
Area: Porta Vittoria
Address: Piazza Adigrat 320133 Milan Italy
Phone: 02 70126312

Milan Shopping Guide / The Most Recommended Stores in the City

---

#361
Details
Category: Shoe Stores
Average Price: Expensive
Area: Fiera
Address: Piazza Piemonte 8
20145 Milan Italy
Phone: 02 43319077

#362
Bershka
Category: Accessories, Women's Clothing
Average Price: Inexpensive
Area: Centro Storico
Address: Via Spadari 1
20123 Milan Italy
Phone: 02 86984449

#363
Nara Camicie
Category: Men's Clothing, Women's Clothing
Average Price: Expensive
Area: Centro Storico
Address: Galleria Vittorio Emanuele 4
20121 Milan Italy
Phone: 02 8752362

#364
Franklin & Marshall
Category: Fashion
Average Price: Modest
Area: Centro Storico
Address: C. Di Porta Ticinese, 76
20123 Milan Italy
Phone: 02 8358730

#365
Gianni Mura
Category: Accessories
Average Price: Modest
Area: Centro Storico
Address: Via Torino, 54
20123 Milan Italy
Phone: 02 72010618

#366
Outlet M.G. Watch
Category: Outlet Stores, Watches, Jewelry
Average Price: Modest
Area: Porta Romana
Address: Via Adige
620135 Milan Italy
Phone: 339 7690222

#367
Kammi Calzature Valassina
Category: Accessories, Shoe Stores
Average Price: Modest
Area: Bovisa
Address: Via Imbriani 61
20158 Milan Italy
Phone: 02 375613

#368
Papillon
Category: Men's Clothing
Average Price: Modest
Area: Fiera
Address: Via Monte Bianco 44
20149 Milan Italy
Phone: 02 468205

#369
Agua Del Carmen
Category: Women's Clothing
Average Price: Modest
Area: Centro Storico
Address: Via Cesare Correnti, 23
20123 Milan Italy
Phone: 02 89415363

#370
Boggi
Category: Accessories, Shoe Stores, Men's Clothing
Average Price: Modest
Area: Buenos Aires
Address: Corso Bueno Aires
20124 Milan Italy
Phone: 02 29526458

#371
Adreani Gioielli
Category: Jewelry Repair, Jewelry
Average Price: Modest
Area: Città Studi
Address: Via L Mangiagalli 520133 Milan Italy
Phone: 02 45487824

#372
Camomilla In Fiore
Category: Fashion
Average Price: Modest
Area: Buenos Aires
Address: Via Degli Scipioni, 1/A
20129 Milan Italy
Phone: 02 29521939

Milan Shopping Guide / The Most Recommended Stores in the City

#373
Petite Therésè
Category: Women's Clothing, Accessories
Average Price: Modest
Area: Porta Romana
Address: Via Col Di Lana 2
20136 Milan Italy
Phone: 02 58105585

#374
Mc Kenzy
Category: Men's Clothing, Women's Clothing
Average Price: Modest
Area: Parco Sempione
Address: Corso Vercelli 2
20145 Milan Italy
Phone: 02 48000666

#375
Zara Home
Category: Home Decor
Average Price: Modest
Area: Centro Storico
Address: Piazza San Babila 5
20122 Milan Italy
Phone: 02 76022740

#376
Miss Miss
Category: Women's Clothing
Average Price: Modest
Area: Palestro
Address: Corso Buenos Aires, 11/42
20124 Milan Italy
Phone: 02 2049174

#377
Oliver's Abbigliamento Uomo
Category: Men's Clothing
Average Price: Modest
Area: Città Studi
Address: Via Vallazze 93
20131 Milan Italy
Phone: 02 70602702

#378
Calzolaio Costanzo
Category: Shoe Repair, Accessories, Shoe Stores
Average Price: Modest
Area: Washington
Address: Via Digione
120144 Milan Italy
Phone: 02 36584673

#379
Casa Milan
Category: Sports Wear, Museums
Average Price: Modest
Area: Fiera
Address: Via Aldo Rossi 8
20149 Milan Italy
Phone: 02 62281

#380
Dmail
Category: Accessories, Home Decor
Average Price: Modest
Area: Centro Storico
Address: Via San Paolo 15
20121 Milan Italy
Phone: 02 86984110

#381
Mango
Category: Women's Clothing, Accessories
Average Price: Modest
Area: Centro Storico
Address: Via Torino 21
20123 Milan Italy
Phone: 02 86990288

#382
H&M
Category: Accessories, Men's Clothing, Women's Clothing
Average Price: Inexpensive
Area: Centro Storico
Address: Galleria Passarella 1
20122 Milan Italy
Phone: 02 76017222

#383
Wag
Category: Fashion
Average Price: Modest
Area: Centro Storico
Address: Via De Amicis 28
20123 Milan Italy
Phone: 02 8053063

#384
OVS
Category: Department Stores
Average Price: Modest
Area: Porta Romana
Address: Corso San Gottardo
3920136 Milan Italy
Phone: 02 8358515

Milan Shopping Guide / The Most Recommended Stores in the City

#385
Alberto Bressan
Category: Shoe Stores
Average Price: Modest
Area: Centro Storico
Address: Corso Di Porta Romana, 54
20122 Milan Italy
Phone: 02 58307390

#386
Gioielleria Pennisi
Category: Jewelry
Average Price: Expensive
Area: Centro Storico
Address: Via Alessandro Manzoni 29
20121 Milan Italy
Phone: 02 862232

#387
C.I.P. Gioielli
Category: Jewelry
Average Price: Inexpensive
Area: Centro Storico
Address: Via Torino 22
20123 Milan Italy
Phone: 02 860333

#388
Penelope Mercatino Dell'usato
Category: Antiques, Thrift Stores, Used, Vintage & Consignment
Average Price: Expensive
Area: Porta Vittoria
Address: Via Macedonio Melloni 6
20129 Milan Italy
Phone: 02 39680588

#389
& Other Stories
Category: Women's Clothing, Accessories
Average Price: Modest
Area: Centro Storico
Address: Corso Vittorio Emanuele 1
20122 Milan Italy
Phone: 02 89096303

#390
Accessorize Nord Italia
Category: Women's Clothing
Average Price: Inexpensive
Area: Centro Storico
Address: Via Torino, 25
20123 Milan Italy
Phone: 02 86457140

#391
Slam Jam Store
Category: Fashion
Average Price: Expensive
Area: Porta Genova
Address: Via Pasquale Paoli, 3/5
20143 Milan Italy
Phone: 02 89424085

#392
Yamamay
Category: Men's Clothing, Women's Clothing
Average Price: Modest
Area: Centro Storico
Address: Corso Di Porta Ticinese 53
20123 Milan Italy
Phone: 06 47786825

#393
Alcott
Category: Men's Clothing, Women's Clothing
Average Price: Modest
Area: Centro Storico
Address: Via Torino 46
20123 Milan Italy
Phone: 02 841351

#394
I Vigna
Category: Furniture Stores, Fabric Stores, Mattresses
Average Price: Modest
Area: Centro Storico
Address: Via Gaudenzio Ferrari 9
20123 Milan Italy
Phone: 02 89402988

#395
Petite Maison
Category: Fashion
Average Price: Modest
Area: Città Studi
Address: Piazzale Susa 11,
20133 Milan Italy
Phone: 02 71040541

#396
Louis Vuitton
Category: Accessories, Luggage
Average Price: Exclusive
Area: Centro Storico
Address: Via Montenapoleone 2
20121 Milan Italy
Phone: 02 7771711

Milan Shopping Guide / The Most Recommended Stores in the City

---

#397
La Fioreria Cuccagna
Category: Gift Shops, Florists
Average Price: Modest
Area: Porta Vittoria
Address: Via Cuccagna 2
20135 Milan Italy
Phone: 02 91637820

#398
Mondi Sommersi
Category: Hobby Shops
Average Price: Modest
Area: Washington
Address: Via Rembrandt Paolo, 9
20148 Milan Italy
Phone: 02 48714184

#399
Stefierre
Category: Accessories, Women's Clothing
Average Price: Modest
Area: Garibaldi
Address: Via Carmagnola 7
20134 Milan Italy
Phone: 02 87390245

#400
Marina Rinaldi
Category: Women's Clothing
Average Price: Expensive
Area: Centro Storico
Address: Piazzetta Del Liberty 2
20121 Milan Italy
Phone: 02 782065

#401
Elda
Category: Accessories, Women's Clothing
Average Price: Modest
Area: Fiera
Address: Piazza Wagner 13
20145 Milan Italy
Phone: 02 4986535

#402
Crazy Import
Category: Antiques
Average Price: Modest
Area: Centro Storico
Address: Via Panzeri 10
20123 Milan Italy
Phone: 02 87392122

#403
Le Stanze Della Memoria
Category: Antiques, Thrift Stores
Average Price: Modest
Area: Palestro
Address: Corso Concordia 9
20129 Milan Italy
Phone: 02 76008692

#404
Spirito Libero RC
Category: Hobby Shops
Average Price: Modest
Area: Certosa
Address: Viale Certosa 99
20151 Milan Italy
Phone: 02 84253813

#405
Burberry
Category: Men's Clothing, Women's Clothing
Average Price: Modest
Area: Centro Storico
Address: Via Montenapoleone 12
20121 Milan Italy
Phone: 02 36010852

#406
Jarret Vintage Shop
Category: Fashion
Average Price: Expensive
Area: Centro Storico
Address: Corso Di Porta Ticinese, 105
20123 Milan Italy
Phone: 02 89055361

#407
BM39
Category: Men's Clothing
Average Price: Modest
Area: Moscova
Address: Corso Como 11
20154 Milan Italy
Phone: 02 29060414

#408
Surimono
Category: Accessories, Home Decor
Average Price: Modest
Area: Centro Storico
Address: Corso Monforte 25
20122 Milan Italy
Phone: 02 76001770

Milan Shopping Guide / The Most Recommended Stores in the City

---

#409
Cade'
Category: Men's Clothing, Accessories
Average Price: Modest
Area: Centro Storico
Address: Galleria Vittorio Emanuele II 5
20121 Milan Italy
Phone: 02 874960

#410
120% Lino
Category: Women's Clothing
Average Price: Exclusive
Area: Moscova
Address: Via Marsala 13
20121 Milan Italy
Phone: 02 76023394

#411
Cielo
Category: Jewelry, Watches
Average Price: Exclusive
Area: Centro Storico
Address: Piazza Del Duomo 19
20121 Milan Italy
Phone: 02 874010

#412
Ardemagni
Category: Leather Goods, Women's Clothing
Average Price: Expensive
Area: Washington
Address: Via Giorgio Washington,
7220146 Milan Italy
Phone: 02 468981

#413
Just Outlet
Category: Outlet Stores
Average Price: Modest
Area: Cinisello Balsamo
Address: Via Edmondo De Amicis 52
20092 Cinisello Balsamo Italy
Phone: 02 61290280

#414
Canadian Outlet
Category: Sports Wear
Average Price: Modest
Area: Parco Sempione
Address: Via Canonica 28
20154 Milan Italy
Phone: 02 33600886

#415
L'Artigiano Di Brera
Category: Shoe Stores
Average Price: Expensive
Area: Centro Storico
Address: Via Solferino 1
20121 Milan Italy
Phone: 02 80581910

#416
PUMA Store
Category: Shoe Stores, Men's Clothing, Women's Clothing
Average Price: Modest
Area: Stazione Centrale
Address: Via Casati 1A
20124 Milan Italy
Phone: 2294 08661

#417
Original Marines
Category: Children's Clothing
Average Price: Modest
Area: Porta Vittoria
Address: Corso XXII Marzo 18
20135 Milan Italy
Phone: 02 54019759

#418
Vitali
Category: Men's Clothing
Average Price: Expensive
Area: Centro Storico
Address: Via Dante
320121 Milan Italy
Phone: 02 8053384

#419
Fornarina
Category: Women's Clothing, Accessories
Average Price: Expensive
Area: Centro Storico
Address: Corso Di Porta Ticinese 78
20123 Milan Italy
Phone: 02 83200759

#420
Bershka Italia
Category: Women's Clothing
Average Price: Modest
Area: Centro Storico
Address: Via Spadari 120123 Milan Italy
Phone: 02 86984449

Milan Shopping Guide / The Most Recommended Stores in the City

---

#421
Il Risveglio Dell'Antico
Category: Gift Shops
Average Price: Expensive
Area: Washington
Address: Via Domenico Cimarosa, 5
20144 Milan Italy
Phone: 02 4692231

#422
Tex Arcobaleno Camicie E Cravatte
Category: Fashion
Average Price: Modest
Area: Porta Vittoria
Address: Via Friuli, 120135 Milan Italy
Phone: 02 55015690

#423
Manila Grace
Category: Women's Clothing
Average Price: Modest
Area: Centro Storico
Address: Via Alessandro Manzoni
4320121 Milan Italy
Phone: 02 62087841

#424
Mango
Category: Women's Clothing, Accessories, Leather Goods
Average Price: Modest
Area: Centro Storico
Address: Corso Vittorio Emanuele II
2420122 Milan Italy
Phone: 02 76014530

#425
Parrucchiere Sif
Category: Hair Salons, Accessories, Cosmetics & Beauty Supply
Average Price: Modest
Area: Ospedale Maggiore
Address: Via Valassina 3520159 Milan Italy
Phone: 02 6883715

#426
Frankie Morello
Category: Men's Clothing, Women's Clothing, Children's Clothing
Average Price: Exclusive
Area: Centro Storico
Address: Corso Matteotti 320121 Milan Italy
Phone: 02 7628115

#427
Cappelleria Cabella
Category: Accessories
Average Price: Modest
Area: Turro Gorla Greco
Address: Viale Monza
2020127 Milan Italy
Phone: 02 26145175

#428
Armeria Excalibur
Category: Fashion
Average Price: Modest
Area: Washington
Address: Via Modestino
320144 Milan Italy
Phone: 02 8323896

#429
Fiordivetro
Category: Jewelry, Gift Shops
Average Price: Modest
Area: Parco Sempione
Address: Via Vincenzo Monti,
3220123 Milan Italy
Phone: 02 48021014

#430
Mondadori Villaggio Barona
Category: Bookstores
Average Price: Modest
Area: Porta Genova
Address: Via Ettore Ponti
2120143 Milan Italy
Phone: 02 39661919

#431
Boutique Malu'
Category: Women's Clothing
Average Price: Modest
Area: Porta Romana
Address: Via Crema, 1
20135 Milan Italy
Phone: 02 58305345

#432
Paladini Abbigliamento
Category: Fashion
Average Price: Modest
Area: Certosa
Address: Via Bodoni Gian Battista
220155 Milan Italy
Phone: 02 33001277

#433
Philipp Plein Showroom
Category: Men's Clothing, Women's Clothing, Children's Clothing
Average Price: Exclusive
Area: Centro Storico
Address: Via Bigli 4
20121 Milan Italy
Phone: 02 87085791

#434
Naviglio Più
Category: Fashion
Average Price: Modest
Area: Porta Genova
Address: Ripa Di Porta Ticinese, 33
20143 Milan Italy
Phone: 02 8373834

#435
Playlife
Category: Fashion
Average Price: Modest
Area: Buenos Aires
Address: Corso Buenos Aires 36
20124 Milan Italy
Phone: 02 20520346

#436
Le Solferine
Category: Shoe Stores
Average Price: Exclusive
Area: Moscova, Centro Storico
Address: Via Solferino 2
20121 Milan Italy
Phone: 02 6555352

#437
Farmacia Santa Teresa
Category: Drugstores
Average Price: Modest
Area: Washington
Address: Corso Magenta
9620123 Milan Italy
Phone: 02 48006772

#438
USA Shop
Category: Fashion
Average Price: Expensive
Area: Centro Storico
Address: Via Torino 7320123 Milan Italy
Phone: 02 86453559

#439
Ab-Side
Category: Women's Clothing
Average Price: Modest
Area: Centro Storico
Address: Vicolo Santa Caterina 1
20122 Milan Italy
Phone: 02 58315234

#440
Civico 82
Category: Shoe Stores, Women's Clothing
Average Price: Expensive
Area: Centro Storico
Address: Corso Di Porta Ticinese, 82
20123 Milan Italy
Phone: 02 89423810

#441
Oltolini Cucine
Category: Home Decor, Kitchen & Bath
Average Price: Modest
Area: Centro Storico
Address: Corso Di Porta Ticinese 89
20123 Milan Italy
Phone: 02 89403510

#442
Onfuton
Category: Home Decor, Furniture Stores
Average Price: Expensive
Area: Porta Romana
Address: Via Crema 14
20135 Milan Italy
Phone: 02 58319894

#443
Modi Atipici
Category: Women's Clothing
Average Price: Modest
Area: Centro Storico
Address: Corso Di Porta Ticinese 66
20123 Milan Italy
Phone: 02 58100206

#444
Mutinelli Cappelli
Category: Accessories
Average Price: Modest
Area: Palestro
Address: Corso Buenos Aires,
520124 Milan Italy
Phone: 02 29523594

Milan Shopping Guide / The Most Recommended Stores in the City

#445
Bettinadue
Category: Women's Clothing, Shoe Stores, Accessories
Average Price: Expensive
Area: Palestro
Address: Via Felice Bellotti 11
20129 Milan Italy
Phone: 02 76004280

#446
Fondazione Prada
Category: Art Galleries, Museums
Average Price: Modest
Area: Porta Romana
Address: Largo Isarco 2
20139 Milan Italy
Phone: 02 56662611

#447
Mugnai Calzature
Category: Shoe Stores
Average Price: Modest
Area: Centro Storico
Address: Corso Italia 18
20122 Milan Italy
Phone: 02 72011498

#448
Il Nascondino
Category: Children's Clothing
Average Price: Inexpensive
Area: Corsica
Address: Via Druso 1
20133 Milan Italy
Phone: 02 78623351

#449
Spectrum
Category: Shoe Stores, Sports Wear
Average Price: Modest
Area: Stazione Centrale
Address: Via Felice Casati 29
20124 Milan Italy
Phone: 02 67071408

#450
Mauro Leone
Category: Shoe Stores
Average Price: Modest
Area: Centro Storico
Address: Via San Pietro All'orto,
920121 Milan Italy
Phone: 02 76022573

#451
D & G Dolce & Gabbana
Category: Fashion
Average Price: Modest
Area: Palestro, Centro Storico
Address: Via Senato, 19
20121 Milan Italy
Phone: 02 799950

#452
Shopping Club
Category: Accessories, Outlet Stores
Average Price: Modest
Area: Cinisello Balsamo
Address: Via Monfalcone 7
20092 Cinisello Balsamo Italy
Phone: 02 36592228

#453
Basile Calzature
Category: Shoe Stores
Average Price: Modest
Area: Porta Vittoria
Address: Via F. Anzani, 2
20135 Milan Italy
Phone: 02 5469256

#454
Grazia Leon
Category: Women's Clothing
Average Price: Modest
Area: Centro Storico
Address: Corso Di Porta Vittoria 50
20122 Milan Italy
Phone: 02 5458090

#455
Swagg
Category: Fashion
Average Price: Modest
Area: Porta Genova
Address: Via Delle Foppette, 2
20144 Milan Italy
Phone: 02 47712816

#456
Biffi Boutique
Category: Accessories, Men's Clothing, Women's Clothing
Average Price: Exclusive
Area: Centro Storico
Address: Corso Genova
620123 Milan Italy
Phone: 02 83116050

Milan Shopping Guide / The Most Recommended Stores in the City

---

#457
Midali
Category: Women's Clothing
Average Price: Expensive
Area: Centro Storico
Address: Corso Di Porta Vittoria, 46
20122 Milan Italy
Phone: 02 55196312

#458
La Casa Della Lana
Category: Fashion
Average Price: Modest
Area: Porta Vittoria
Address: C. Ventidue Marzo, 28
20135 Milan Italy
Phone: 02 59901138

#459
Bagutta
Category: Fashion
Average Price: Modest
Area: Centro Storico
Address: Via Fiori Chiari 7
20121 Milan Italy
Phone: 02 89013498

#460
Rocca
Category: Watches, Jewelry
Average Price: Exclusive
Area: Centro Storico
Address: Piazza Del Duomo 25
20122 Milan Italy
Phone: 02 8057447

#461
Midali
Category: Women's Clothing
Average Price: Expensive
Area: Centro Storico
Address: C. Di Porta Ticinese, 87
20123 Milan Italy
Phone: 02 89406830

#462
Anna Lenti
Category: Women's Clothing
Average Price: Modest
Area: Porta Vittoria
Address: Via Pietro Calvi 2
20129 Milan Italy
Phone: 02 76017442

#463
Maclù
Category: Fashion
Average Price: Modest
Area: Porta Romana
Address: Viale Col Di Lana, 2
20136 Milan Italy
Phone: 02 58107754

#464
Borsalino
Category: Accessories
Average Price: Modest
Area: Centro Storico
Address: Corso Venezia, 21/A
20121 Milan Italy
Phone: 02 2046396

#465
Womo
Category: Accessories, Lingerie
Average Price: Exclusive
Area: Centro Storico
Address: Via Dante 4
20121 Milan Italy
Phone: 02 89096163

#466
Calzedonia
Category: Women's Clothing
Average Price: Modest
Area: Certosa
Address: Via Grosotto 7
20149 Milan Italy
Phone: 02 39273219

#467
Runner Store
Category: Sports Wear, Shoe Stores
Average Price: Modest
Area: Bande Nere
Address: Viale Delle Legioni Romane
5920147 Milan Italy
Phone: 02 48376605

#468
Calzature Gallon
Category: Shoe Stores
Average Price: Inexpensive
Area: Centro Storico
Address: Via Piazza S. Eustorgio, 4
20122 Milan Italy
Phone: 02 89402735

Milan Shopping Guide / The Most Recommended Stores in the City

#469
Spazio Casa Teatro
Category: Art Galleries
Average Price: Modest
Area: Porta Genova
Address: Via Tortona 14
20144 Milan Italy
Phone: 02 36532885

#470
Celestino Manieri
Category: Leather Goods
Average Price: Modest
Area: Porta Romana
Address: Corso S. Gottardo 8
20142 Milan Italy
Phone: 02 89409953

#471
Mauro Bolognesi
Category: Antiques
Average Price: Expensive
Area: Porta Genova
Address: Ripa Di Porta Ticinese 47
20143 Milan Italy
Phone: 333 2282602

#472
Capozzo Daniela
Category: Fashion
Average Price: Modest
Area: Città Studi
Address: Via Antonio Bazzini 1
20131 Milan Italy
Phone: 02 70600849

#473
Yoox
Category: Discount Store
Average Price: Modest
Area: Porta Genova
Address: Via Morimondo 17
20143 Milan Italy
Phone: 02 83112811

#474
Hogan Headquarter
Category: Fashion
Average Price: Modest
Area: Porta Genova
Address: Via Savona 56
20144 Milan Italy
Phone: 02 77225700

#475
Porselli
Category: Shoe Stores
Average Price: Expensive
Area: Centro Storico
Address: Piazza Paolo Ferrari 6
20121 Milan Italy
Phone: 02 8053759

#476
Kasanova
Category: Home Decor,
Appliances, Gift Shops
Average Price: Modest
Area: Centro Storico
Address: Via Mercato 26
20121 Milan Italy
Phone: 02 89095229

#477
Ader
Category: Men's Clothing
Average Price: Expensive
Area: Moscova
Address: Via Della Moscova, 52
20121 Milan Italy
Phone: 02 29062425

#478
Mary Cadeaux
Category: Arts & Crafts, Jewelry, Gift Shops
Average Price: Modest
Area: Garibaldi
Address: Via Valtellina, 40
20159 Milan Italy
Phone: 02 6682841

#479
The Cuir
Category: Leather Goods
Average Price: Modest
Area: Palestro
Address: Via Spallanzani 1820129 Milan Italy
Phone: 02 29531824

#480
J.D.C. Urban Store
Category: Men's Clothing
Average Price: Modest
Area: Centro Storico
Address: Piazza Del Duomo,
3120122 Milan Italy
Phone: 02 86461737

Milan Shopping Guide / The Most Recommended Stores in the City

---

#481
La Bottega Del Sarto
Category: Men's Clothing, Accessories
Average Price: Modest
Area: Centro Storico
Address: Corso Genova 6
20123 Milan Italy
Phone: 02 58108893

#482
Daniela E Andrea
Category: Women's Clothing
Average Price: Modest
Area: Porta Vittoria
Address: Corso Lodi 7
20135 Milan Italy
Phone: 02 55184902

#483
Casabella Milano
Category: Kitchen & Bath, Home Decor
Average Price: Exclusive
Area: Washington
Address: Via Vincenzo Foppa, 50/A
20144 Milan Italy
Phone: 02 474431

#484
Segreti
Category: Women's Clothing
Average Price: Modest
Area: Porta Romana
Address: Corso San Gottardo, 13
20136 Milan Italy
Phone: 02 58110670

#485
Wot - Waste Of Time
Category: Comic Books, Fashion, Arcades
Average Price: Modest
Area: Porta Romana
Address: Via Adige 7
20135 Milan Italy
Phone: 02 49756000

#486
Calvin Klein Underwear
Category: Men's Clothing, Women's Clothing
Average Price: Expensive
Area: Palestro
Address: Corso Buenos Aires
20124 Milan Italy
Phone: 0039 0229532164

#487
Let's Cake
Category: Home Decor
Average Price: Modest
Area: Città Studi
Address: Via Porpora 5
20131 Milan Italy
Phone: 340 7174560

#488
Nobleman
Category: Fashion
Average Price: Modest
Area: Washington
Address: Via Solari 43
20144 Milan Italy
Phone: 02 428696

#489
Camiceria Olga
Category: Sewing & Alterations, Men's Clothing, Women's Clothing
Average Price: Modest
Area: Porta Vittoria
Address: Via Comelico 3
20135 Milan Italy
Phone: 02 45478092

#490
Progetto G
Category: Women's Clothing
Average Price: Modest
Area: Fiera
Address: Via Belfiore 2
20145 Milan Italy
Phone: 02 4817478

#491
House Of Cashmere Mayfair
Category: Fashion
Average Price: Modest
Area: Centro Storico
Address: Via Nirone, 220123 Milan Italy
Phone: 02 86453404

#492
Muji
Category: Home Decor
Average Price: Expensive
Area: Garibaldi
Address: Piazza Gae Aulenti
20124 Milan Italy
Phone: 02 66983849

Milan Shopping Guide / The Most Recommended Stores in the City

#493
Il Salotto Di Antonella
Category: Men's Clothing, Women's Clothing
Average Price: Modest
Area: Centro Storico
Address: Via Urbano III
320123 Milan Italy
Phone: 393 9588301

#494
Marco
Category: Shoe Stores
Average Price: Modest
Area: Porta Vittoria
Address: Corso XXII Marzo,
820135 Milan Italy
Phone: 02 59901292

#495
Peter Pan
Category: Cards & Stationery,
Printing Services
Average Price: Modest
Area: Fiera
Address: Via Francesco Albani 69
20148 Milan Italy
Phone: 02 33001139

#496
Ricami Veronica
Category: Accessories
Average Price: Modest
Area: Washington
Address: Corso Vercelli,
Angolo Via Cherubini,
420145 Milan Italy
Phone: 02 48013173

#497
Cartoleria Tre Ponti
Category: Toy Stores, Cards & Stationery
Average Price: Modest
Area: Corsica
Address: Via Facchinetti 2
20138 Milan Italy
Phone: 02 7385949

#498
Anna
Category: Women's Clothing, Men's Clothing
Average Price: Modest
Area: Washington
Address: Via Washington Giorgio 82
20146 Milan Italy
Phone: 02 4239063

#499
Chacha
Category: Jewelry, Arts &
Crafts, Women's Clothing
Average Price: Modest
Area: Centro Storico
Address: Via Cesare Correnti
1920123 Milan Italy
Phone: 02 83242251

#500
JDC
Category: Women's Clothing,
Men's Clothing, Accessories
Average Price: Modest
Area: Palestro
Address: Corso Buenos Aires
620124 Milan Italy
Phone: 02 45395810

Milton Keynes UK
Ingram Content Group UK Ltd.
UKHW010857030424
440506UK00016B/2203